Healing From a Cheating Spouse

Guides On How to Start All Over Again From a Broken Marriage

Joyce Mendez

All rights reserved. No part
of this publication may be
reproduced, distributed, or
transmitted in any form or by
any means, including
photocopying, recording, or
other electronic or
mechanical methods, without
the prior written permission
of the publisher, except in
the case of brief quotations

embodied in critical reviews and certain other noncommercial uses permitted by copyright law. Copyright © by [Joyce Mendez] 2022

Table of Contents

Chapter 1
What is Infidelity in Marriage?

Infidelity (synonyms
include cheating, straying, adultery, being unfaithful, two-
timing, or having an affair) is a violation of a couple's
emotional and/or sexual exclusivity that commonly results
in feelings of anger, sexual jealousy, and rivalry.

What constitutes infidelity depends on expectations within
the relationship. In marital relationships, exclusivity is
commonly assumed. Infidelity can cause psychological
damage, including feelings of rage and betrayal, low
sexual and personal confidence, and even post-traumatic
stress disorder.[1] People of all genders can experience social
consequences if their act of infidelity becomes public, but
the form and extent of these consequences can depend on
the gender of the unfaithful person.

Infidelity can be best explained as any action that violates
an implicit or explicit agreement between two people, thus
harming a relationship. What might begin as friendship or
compassionate connection increases over a while and
becomes an intimate relationship. Often, platonic
friendships evolve into emotional affairs, and the line
between these two types of relationships runs very thin.
Platonic friendship turns into an affair when it becomes
emotionally intimate and involves some level of secrecy.

Now, most of you would section infidelity into a physical realm, one that only includes sexual contact with someone other than the person they're committed or married to.

Infidelity is certainly one of the major reason that has led to the destruction of marriages. Infidelity is also one of the legal grounds for divorce, besides living separately for more than a year and subjecting your partner to cruelty (either mental or physical).

Of course, there are people who forgive their spouses and continue living their marriage, maybe for the sake of children or their dependency on their partners.

But, not everybody is able to get over the hurt caused by their cheating partner.

There are many people who are unwilling to give a second chance to their partner. This situation inevitably leads to legal separation.

The consequences of infidelity are numerous, and it is only natural to want to know why your partner chose to cheat, even if knowing why doesn't bring you any relief. There could be any number of reasons, and there are many types of infidelity and cheating that could shed a little light on those reasons.

Each case of infidelity is different and fulfills a different need. Although knowing why a partner cheated likely won't lessen any pain you feel, being able to rationalize the behavior and define it will alleviate some confusion. It can also help you feel more confident in how to move forward from the situation—whether that means working on healing your relationship or moving on should you decide to split up.

Learn more about the five types of cheating below, and what to do if you find yourself the victim of infidelity.

Opportunistic Infidelity

Opportunistic infidelity occurs when one is in love and attached to their partner, but succumbs to their sexual desire for someone else. Typically, this type of cheating is driven by situational circumstances or opportunity, risk-taking behavior, and alcohol or drug use. As social psychologist Theresa E. DiDonato says, "Not every act of infidelity is premeditated and driven by dissatisfaction with a current relationship…Maybe they were drinking or in some other way thrown into an opportunity they didn't anticipate."

After the fact, the more in love a person is with their partner, the more guilt they will experience as a result of their sexual encounter. However, feelings of guilt tend to fade as the fear of being caught subsides.

Obligatory Infidelity

This type of infidelity is based on the fear that resisting someone's sexual advances will result in rejection. People may have feelings of sexual desire, love, and attachment for a partner, but still, <u>end up cheating</u> because they have a strong need for approval. In addition, their need for approval can cause them to act in ways that

are at odds with their other feelings. In other words, some people cheat, not because they want to cheat, but because they need the approval that comes along with having the attention of others.

Romantic Infidelity

"Sometimes (but not always) a deficit in an existing relationship leads people to have extra dyadic affairs," says DiDonato. This type of infidelity occurs when the cheater has little <u>emotional attachment</u> to their partner. They may be committed to their marriage and making it work, but they long for an intimate, loving connection with someone else. More than likely, their commitment to the marriage will prevent them from ever leaving their spouse. Romantic infidelity means pain for the other man or woman and the cheating partner—rarely does it turn into a long-term, committed relationship. Marital problems have to be quite severe before a spouse will leave the marriage for another person.

Conflicted Romantic Infidelity

This type of infidelity occurs when people experience genuine love and sexual **desire for more than one person** at a time. Despite our idealistic notions of having only one true love, it is possible to experience intense romantic love for multiple people at the same time. While such situations are emotionally possible, they are very complicated and tend to create a lot of anxiety and stress. In this case, cheating partners, in their attempt not to cause anyone harm, often end up hurting everyone.

Commemorative Infidelity

This type of infidelity occurs when a person is in a committed relationship but has no feelings for their partner. There is no sexual desire or love or attachment, only a sense of obligation keeping the couple together. "Lacking love and lacking commitment to a current romantic partner are both tied to general feelings of relationship dissatisfaction," says DiDonato.

These people justify cheating by telling themselves they have the right to look for what they are not getting in their present relationship. Unfulfilled sexual desires can easily come into play here. "Maybe in their established relationship, individuals aren't engaging in the frequency of sex, style of sex, or specific sexual behaviors that they want," DiDonato adds. "This can contribute to their reasons to cheat."

Now that your confusion has hopefully been alleviated, it's up to you to decide what steps to take next. Marriages and relationships can survive infidelity, but whether or not yours survives will depend on what type of infidelity took place and how much work you're both willing to put in. It's only common sense to know that an opportunistic cheater will cheat regardless of how many times their cheating is discovered and forgiven. That said, any other reasons why your spouse cheated don't mean they won't cheat again, so keep that in mind when deciding what steps to take next.

Chapter 2

Things that leads to Infidelity

Before we discuss the glaring causes of infidelity in relationships, let us look at how common infidelity is in committed relationships.Sexual infidelity is undoubted a massive threat to the stability of a committed relationship and is indeed one of the hardest ones to overcome.

A research paper suggests that around one-third of men and one-quarter of women might get involved in extradyadic sexual relationships at the minimum once in their lifetime. As we know, the concept of infidelity is not just restricted to the realms of physical intimacy; people engage in emotional affairs. So, we can only imagine the numbers! Also, as per research, 70% of all Americans get involved in some kind of affair during their marital life. By referring to these statistics, we can infer that infidelity is way too common than we perceive it to be.

The implications of infidelity on relationships are severe. So, it is better to be aware of the various causes of infidelity to avert the problems well in advance.

Marriage and infidelity' is an extremely distressing combination. But, what causes infidelity in marriage? According to experts, one of the most common causes of infidelity is a sense of emotional disconnection from your partner.

As per research from the American Association for Marriage and Family Therapy, 35 percent of women and 45 percent of men have had emotional affairs outside

heir primary relationship. The person who has committed adultery complains of feeling unappreciated, unloved, ignored, and overall sadness or feeling of insecurity, leading them to cheat on their partner. However, there have also been cases where only the thrill of doing something secretive and tasting the forbidden fruit lead to infidelity.

There are numerous causes of infidelity, and each case is different from the other.

While some believe that it is the result of a loveless marriage, others believe that it results from a hasty decision that cannot be undone. Others believe that infidelity is nothing but a failure to work out relationship problems.

Having said that, let us have a look at some of the commonly observed causes of infidelity. The internet has become one of the significant facilitators of infidelity.

It is very easy to get connected with people and continue talking to them for hours at length whether you are at home, work, or even in some public place. There are many websites where people can meet up, leading to the beginning of a new relationship.

Inability to deal with problems

Running away from problems and the inability to deal with them is a major cause of infidelity. There are times when instead of dealing with the problem at hand, husbands or wives end up making excuses and try to find some other way that opens the door to infidelity. There have been many examples where a spouse reported that they found a coworker with whom they could share their problems and feel comfortable, which was the beginning of the affair.

It comes as no surprise that most infidelity cases occur in workplaces where sympathetic coworkers offered a shoulder to lean on.

Porn addiction

Porn content is very readily available on the internet, and this is one of the major causes of infidelity and destroyed relationships these days.

The Internet makes pornography widely available. You have to go online and type in a search in Google. It's that easy.

Watching porn from time to time can seem innocent, but the long-term effects are rather harmful. Porn addiction is thus one of the top reasons for infidelity in relationships.

If you feel that you are getting addicted, make sure that you monitor your addiction and dissuade yourself from getting too much into the habit.

Alcohol or drug addiction

Alcohol or drug addiction is also one of the common causes of infidelity in relationships. Often addiction makes a person get into detrimental habits like lying, stealing, and even cheating.

Overconsumption of alcohol or drugs causes people to lose their inhibitions and behave irrationally. In turn, people can easily give in to temporary feelings of infatuation and drift away from their partners.

Boredom

You might not believe it, but boredom is one of the leading causes of infidelity. People fall into routines that take the excitement from their lives, including their bedroom lives.

This often leads to cheating when one partner is no longer satisfied in the relationship and seeks something new and thrilling. Many people look for excitement to escape boredom and experiment with various things like adopting new hobbies or hanging out with different people. They end up cheating their partners even without meaning to do so.

Lack of healthy relations

Lack of normal or healthy relations is also one of the key causes of infidelity. There are couples who have married for a certain reason, or they are staying together for certain motives like children or financial issues, but there is no

love between them, and they cannot tolerate being with each other more than needed.

There are also situations where people ignore their spouses. They don't live like a normal couple, go out together, have a passionate relationship, and ultimately one or both of them look outside their relationship for someone whom they want to be with.

The feeling of being unwanted

Some people try to seek love out of their primary relationship because they feel that their partners no longer want them. This often results when one partner is living a very successful and busy life and does not have time for their spouse. When the other spouse starts feeling like their opinion and feelings don't matter, they counteract the strong undesired influence of cheating. In their heads, this act will bring back their dignity and self-esteem. They want to show that they're still there and they're still worth it in somebody else's eyes. If you notice such a misbalance in your relationship, try to think of ways to grow towards each other as equals. Otherwise, you might end up in a mess that you both regret later on.

Living apart for a long time

Although distance doesn't matter in true love, living apart for a long time is one of the most common causes of infidelity. Often, couples are forced to stay apart from

each other due to their job's nature and work commitments. When one partner is absent for a long time, the other partner is lonely, and to keep themselves busy, they find new activities that might involve interacting with other people where they get a little too involved with someone.

Couples also drift apart when they spend too much time away from each other, and they no longer feel connected or attached as before. They either fall in love with someone else or simply resort to infidelity to make up for the emptiness.

Sweet revenge

What happens when one of the partners resorts to cheating in a relationship?

There are precisely two scenarios– either the relationship falls apart immediately, or the sin is forgiven, and the couple moves on. But you've got to be careful as this sounds too good to be true!

Often one claims to have forgiven, but they'll never forget cheating in a relationship.

The person who was initially hurt might have an affair only to reclaim their own sense of value. After all, romantic revenge does exist! So, after the transgression, it is even possible that the partners call it even. A different matter is whether this relationship will last any longer!

When the partner behaves more like a child

Suppose one of the partners has to take care of everything in the household, make all the critical decisions, or provide the family budget. In that case, they might start feeling as they're a parent instead of a significant other. This is one of the primary reasons why spouses cheat.

As they cannot find the desired balance within their relationship, they subconsciously start looking for it somewhere else. And, as soon as they find somebody who appears to be their equal, they'll be prone to cheating in a relationship.

Issues involving body image/ Aging

People stop chasing their partners after getting married or getting committed in a relationship.

The 'chasing' or the 'honeymoon' period is pretty brief, and as time progresses, it becomes easy to take each other for granted.

Often this lackadaisical approach leads you to neglect how you look and carry yourself. By no means, we endorse physical appearance as a parameter to be loved.

But, unfortunately, there are times when people start missing the older, appealing version of their partners and look for easy replacements instead.

Lack of respect and appreciation

Sometimes partners feel that they are not respected and appreciated enough in the relationship, which ultimately fuels marital discord.

In turn, the disgruntled partners often try to fill the void by seeking solace in some other person's company. And, in no time, they might crossover the boundaries of healthy friendship and resort to infidelity.

So, never miss out on these two ingredients- respect and appreciation, if you wish to see your relationship going a long way.

Unfulfilled sexual desires

Unfulfilled sexual desire is one of the glaring causes of infidelity.

 As per a study published in The Normal Bar, 52% of people who were dissatisfied with their sex lives are more likely to give in to the outside attraction as compared to only 17% of those who were sexually satisfied in their primary relationships.

It implies that people who do not have a fulfilling sex life are three times as likely to cheat on their partners as compared to those with pleasurable intimacy levels.

Also, there are people who claim that 'My sex drive is too high to be handled by one person.' Of course, by no means is this a legitimate reason for cheating your partner. But in the same study as mentioned above, 46% of men and 19% of

women cited it as a reason for their affair. So, if you find yourself grappling with issues in your sex life, it would be best if you could try considering sex therapy instead of opting for infidelity.

When a partner wants to sabotage a relationship

Cheating in a relationship also occurs when a partner is not just happy in a relationship but also wants to sabotage it before breaking up.

This could be a sheer case of vengeance when a partner, for some reason, wishes to inflict pain on the other before leaving.

At the same time, it's also possible that the person resorting to cheating in a relationship wants to end it but wanting the other person to initiate. In such cases, the cheating partner wants to get caught and expects the other partner to break up with them.

Falling out of love with your partner

You may call it falling out of love with your partner or falling in love with someone else. Although you might find this reason to be insignificant to cause infidelity, this is one of the reasons why people cheat. Often, you might not be able to fathom the real reason behind falling out of love. However, there have been instances wherein people happen to grow apart and fall out of love.

Chapter 3

How to find out that your partner is cheating

If you've ever noticed signs of cheating coming from your partner, then you likely know the awful, gut-wrenching feeling that something isn't right. Signs of a cheating husband or wife can be large or small, obvious or subtle. It doesn't help that identifying and making sense of these indicators is usually difficult, thanks to the emotions involved and the fact that cheating "isn't always black and white," explains Samantha Burns, L.M.H.C., couples therapist and author of Breaking Up and Bouncing Back. "Cheating can be both physical and emotional, and involves breaking the covert or overt boundaries of your relationship."

"Since cheating is cloaked in secrecy, the person is doing their best not to arouse suspicion in their partner," says licensed marriage and family therapist Lesli Doares, author of *Blueprint for a Lasting Marriage*. "The cheater's goal is to not get caught and then have to deal with the consequences. They strive to make everything appear normal."

At the same time, people tend to draw conclusions about their partner based on their pre-existing beliefs, says psychologist Paul Coleman, Psy.D., author of *Finding Peace When Your Heart Is In Pieces*. So if you tend to be a trusting person, it can be easy to mistake the less-obvious signs of cheating for more harmless red flags instead.

Keep an out for these warning signs below; noticing just one may not be a surefire sign of an unfaithful partner, but if you check multiple off this list, it may be time to have a vulnerable chat. After all, if they have nothing to hide, they should be more than happy to put your fears to rest.

They're suddenly unreachable.

Again, a change is the big factor. If your partner has a job that makes it tough to reach them during certain hours of the day, it doesn't mean they're cheating. But if

you're suddenly struggling to reach them when you could in the past, and it's a consistent issue, that should raise a red flag.

"Cheaters need privacy and blocks of uninterrupted time," Coleman points out. "Someone engaged in an ongoing affair must be periodically unreachable." After all, they don't want to risk you hearing suspicious voices or background noises

Their schedule changes with no good explanation.

Most people have predictable schedules, and even if their schedule changes, there's usually a reason that makes sense. "Someone who must 'work late' all of a sudden at times that go beyond a reasonable explanation may be cheating," Coleman says.

That's especially true if this keeps happening when your partner has no new job, promotion, or project they're working on.

Their friends don't seem as friendly as they used to be.

Cheaters tend to be less careful about covering their tracks in front of friends versus you. And, of course, people tend to confide in their friends. As a result, "there is a good chance your partner's friends may know what's really going on before you do," Coleman says. Those friends may end up feeling uneasy and anxious around you because they know something you don't.

They have a decrease—or increase—in libido.

It's more common for cheaters to decrease the frequency of sex at home, given that they're getting it elsewhere, Coleman says. But sometimes they try to have sex _more_ at home. "Guilt-ridden people may increase lovemaking," Coleman says. "Some will do so to cover their tracks. But some may do so to satisfy a partner so that the partner will not be seeking sex at a later time when the cheater knows he or she won't be available."

They're suddenly paying more attention to their appearance.

Sometimes people decide to focus on their appearance as part of a New Year's resolution or choose to start a new fitness routine for health reasons—but they're usually pretty open about it.

"The reasons and timing must make sense," Coleman says. If your partner is suddenly wearing cologne or spending a lot of money on new clothes, and it was never their thing in the past, it's "not unreasonable to inquire why," Coleman says. If their answer doesn't make sense, it should raise a red flag.

Their phone habits change.

This can include a range of things, like changing their password or keeping their phone on them all the time when they used to leave it sitting out."

In committed partnerships, it's not uncommon to know your partner's password or be able to pick up their phone to look something up on the internet or snap a cute picture if your phone isn't nearby," says Burns. "If your partner seems possessive over their phone, or gets mad when you ask to use it, they may be hiding something."

They're engaging in suspicious activity on social media.

Social media behaviors such as following provocative accounts or people they don't know, or engaging with suggestive posts may be a warning sign of cheating, but is also a behavior that falls into a "gray area of infidelity" in itself, Burns explains.

If you mention your concern to your partner and they "belittle you, or tell you that you're being too sensitive, this is a red flag that they don't respect you and will likely keep doing these behaviors," says Burns. Additionally, continued behavior of this type sometimes becomes a "slippery slope" that leads to an affair.

They just seem to be around less than usual.

Cheaters have to make time for their fling—and that time usually comes from time you once spent together. "Also, if the affair has gone on for a while, there may be demands placed upon them by their paramour to spend more time together," Coleman says.

Again, it's perfectly OK and expected to ask your partner what's going on when they're suddenly not around as much as usual.

What they say and what actually happens does not add up.

"This is often how cheaters get caught," Doares says. Maybe your partner says they needed to do something that doesn't add up, or someone they say they were with slips that they weren't. "The truth is easy but lies are hard to keep straight," she says. "Objective evidence supports truth but often conflicts with lies."

They don't disclose details of their day anymore.

People usually share intimate details of their day with their partner. But when they're cheating, that tends to shift to the new fling, Mayer says. As a result, they end up telling you less. Remember: "In committed relationships it is normal to tell your partner where you'll be, who will be there, and what time you're expecting to be home," Burns explains. "If your partner is dodging these questions, or you find out they aren't where they said they'd be or with someone different, then your suspicions might be justified."

They get defensive when you ask why certain things have changed.

Relationships change and evolve, but this should be something you can talk about as a couple. "If there is an innocent explanation for why some things have changed there is no need for defensiveness," Coleman says. A cheater may answer a question with a question, like "Why do you ask?" or "Why is that important?" because they need more time to come up with an answer they can get away with, he says.

They start giving you more gifts than usual.

Of course, loving partners give gifts. But cheaters take this to the next level to cover their tracks, Coleman says. It can be a way of reassuring you that they love you and are devoted to you "so that any subtle sign of cheating the partner uncovers can be readily dismissed as something 'they would never do,'" he says.

The relationship issues you've had in the past don't seem to be there anymore.

Every couple has some kind of issue that keeps surfacing. If it suddenly goes away, and there seems to be no reason for it, you should be concerned.

"This can be a sign of cheating or just that your partner has given up trying and is looking for a way out," Doares says. A big sign that something is off with this: The tension isn't there anymore, but you don't feel connected either.

They accuse *You* of cheating.

This is a weird but common habit of cheaters—and there are a few reasons for it, Coleman says. By making your alleged behavior the issue, it puts you on the defensive and takes the focus off of them. It can also make you less likely to speak up about things that seem off because you don't want to upset them, given that they're already "worried" that you're cheating. And it also gives them a reason to say they need "time away to think," a.k.a. meet up with their lover.

You just have a gut feeling.

"In general, if your gut, a.k.a your intuition, is telling you something is wrong, it usually is," Burns notes. "Our intuition is a superpower for survival that picks up on tiny clues or sensing when something feels off, so if this warning bell is going off in your body, then pay attention!" In a healthy relationship your partner should listen and be understanding when you raise your concerns, and work with you to help ease your fears and feel more secure moving forward.

Bottom line: If your partner is showing any of these signs, or things just don't feel right to you, it's perfectly acceptable to ask what's going on, Mayer says. Hopefully, there's a perfectly reasonable explanation.

How to deal with signs of cheating

If you notice signs of a cheating partner or have solid evidence of cheating, your emotional response may make it difficult to confront your partner, but it's important these feelings (and your partner's behaviors) are addressed. Find a calm moment to speak with your partner about your concerns and give them a chance to do the same, and offer an explanation for their behaviors, real or perceived. "Communication is key for the success of any relationship," Burns explains. "If they get defensive, blame you, or focus angrily on how you obtained this

information, this is a red flag that your partner won't be honest, won't take accountability, or won't put in the work to repair the relationship."

If your suspicions of cheating are confirmed, you'll have to make an important decision about the future of the relationship. There's no one correct answer, but it's worth noting that depending on the circumstances "couples can absolutely come out stronger on the other side of infidelity," Burns says. "It requires a lot of work and communication, usually aided by couples therapy and individual therapy," which will help you both learn to heal and rebuild trust.

Chapter Four

When the Cheating Spouse doesn't want a divorce

Having cheated on their husbands, many women have absolutely no intention to dissolve the marriage and ruin their families.

To understand why your cheating wife doesn't want a divorce, you need to identify the root cause of her adulterous behavior. Only then can you decide how to handle the situation.

Infidelity is not rare in our society. Study shows that approximately 28% of people have cheated on their partners. Interestingly, women in the survey were unfaithful in 31.4% of cases, compared to 24% of men.

So, let's dig deeper to decide what to do if your wife cheated but doesn't want a divorce.

Why a Wife Doesn't Want to Divorce

We've heard a lot about situations when a husband cheated but doesn't want a divorce. But many women who have an affair also don't want to leave their marriage. It may sound strange, mostly because society believes that men's infidelity has little connection to love for the other woman.

In contrast, the women's infidelity includes a strong romantically interest in their new partner.

But why don't they want to divorce, then?

The idea of divorce might be frightening to your cheating wife because of several things. So, let's inspect some of the possible reasons she wants to avoid divorce.

She can't afford to live alone

A wife may be used to the financial security that the marriage provides. Ideally, spouses have a joint bank account, family insurance, and tax benefits for being married. However, if a cheating spouse divorces her husband, she will need more money than she currently has to her name. Housing costs are rising every year, making it challenging to live alone. Even with financial support that a husband could provide as alimony and child support, it would be challenging to survive.

In 2020, 18.7% of single-mother families lived below the poverty level, according to Statista.com. So, a wife may not want a divorce to save herself and the kids from financial difficulties

She wants the children to grow up with both parents

A wife can openly say, "I cheated, but I don't want a divorce because of the children." Maybe she even got married because she was pregnant, and her child needed a two-parent family. After all, if the spouse is a mother, she would want to protect her kids' feelings and well-being.

However, it is more prevalent these days to believe that having both parents is not as important to a child's mental health as a conflict-free environment at home between parents. Children will have more adverse mental effects in the short and long term if they live in high-conflict families, writes Ann Gold Buscho Ph.D. in her article for Psychology Today.

So, after divorce, children will be more or less okay if their parents can maintain a civilized relationship.

Divorce is too expensive

If you know how much money a divorce costs, you understand why a cheating spouse doesn't want to rush to hire a divorce attorney. Contested divorces are usually the most expensive.

Depending on the amount of property and the presence of underage children, the cost may reach $10,000-$12,000. A simple consultation with a lawyer where you talk about your possible divorce options will not be cheap. The average hourly rate for an attorney is between $100-$500. An uncontested divorce is less expensive. If you hire a lawyer to review the divorce settlement, you'll pay a few thousand dollars at most. Spouses can also use self-help options to reduce the cost of divorce.

However, a couple would need to talk to each other about it. A peaceful divorce includes both sides agreeing on certain things, and, sometimes, the husband and wife would need a mediator to facilitate the negotiation.

She is comfortable in the current situation
Most people won't change anything if they are comfortable. That's why a spouse stays in the family and doesn't want a divorce. Ending a marriage is always accompanied by changes and new life paths for all family members. For this reason, some spouses prefer to remain in a familiar environment rather than start from scratch. Divorce also means making your own decisions and solving many issues simultaneously, for example, where to live, which parent will keep the children, what happens with insurance, etc. Perhaps a cheating spouse does not want to get divorced because she is not ready to deal with these issues and get used to a new way of life.

Her new fling is unreliable

It's a rare thing when a wife cheats and doesn't care whether her husband finds out. Most of the time, they try to hide it. But why not come clean and get it over with? Maybe the wife knows that her new partner is not ready to commit. So, she doesn't want a divorce because she has nowhere to go. Plus, the person she is having an affair with might be taken (married or in another relationship) and is not ready to ditch their other romantic partner.

Can You Get Divorced without the Wife's Consent?

It is possible if the wife is not pregnant at the time of filing for divorce. Therefore, the husband will have to wait until after the baby is born in some states, even if he

thinks it's not his. In other circumstances, a person doesn't need their wife's consent to start a divorce process. There is a specific procedure for a spouse to end their marriage. First, they have to file a divorce petition with the court. Infidelity is one of the grounds to end a marriage, along with cruelty (e.g., domestic violence) or abandonment.

So, a petitioner may check the "adultery" square in the document and take it to their local court.

However, if the wife had an affair, and the husband wants a divorce, but she doesn't, the divorce process might get messy. Each spouse will probably need a lawyer to handle contentious issues and provide specific advice on how to get a better outcome.

Hiring a divorce attorney is absolutely necessary if a couple has children but can't agree on child custody issues.

How Does Infidelity Affect the Divorce Outcome?

If you're in the mode of "my wife cheated on me, and I want a divorce," you should be aware of what consequences your spouse's adultery can have for the divorce outcome. The primary things to consider are property, child custody, and spousal support. Some of these could tilt in the husband's favor if the wife cheated during the marriage.

Should I Keep Living With a Cheating Spouse?

If your wife has cheated and you're still pondering over the question "Should I divorce my cheating wife?" this section will help you look at things more clearly.

It is difficult to find an excuse for the affair, but it is worth understanding the reasons before deciding to divorce a cheating spouse.

Kenneth P. Rosenberg, MD, distinguishes three main factors that contribute to infidelity:

- Physiological (brain structure and chemistry in the body).

- Psychological (your way of thinking and self-perception).

- Cultural (e.g., opportunities for affairs).

Perhaps the affair was the result of circumstances. For example, the husband had to take an extended business trip abroad or was imprisoned, etc. Also, "affairs can give people a sense of achievement, adventure, romance, intimacy, and sexual variety," Deborah L. Rhode wrote in her book 'Adultery: Infidelity and the Law.'

Other reasons include loss of interest in the husband, a high level of sex hormones, the influence of friends who accept adulterous behavior, and so on.

If you realize that your wife cheats because she doesn't love you anymore, maybe it's not a good idea to stay together.

Be completely honest with yourself and imagine how your life with the same person would look after you decide to forgive them. Remember that nothing will be as it was before your wife cheated.

If you and your spouse are ready to experience many changes, you still have hope to make your marriage work.

Chapter Five
Visiting a marriage counsellor/therapist

Recovery from infidelity can depend on cultural background. It may depend on a couple's personal or religious views. Many couples pursue therapy to decide if they should stay in a

relationship after the affair.
Therapy may help them process
their feelings about it.

A therapist can be a supportive
listener. They can listen as both
parties share how they feel about
the infidelity. A therapist can
help the couple learn about their
needs and relationship goals. The
couple may then choose to
maintain or end their
relationship. A therapist can help
if the couple wishes to save the
relationship. They may help the
couple learn how committed they
are to the relationship. The
partners may learn to
repair trust and navigate the
healing process.

A therapist can also help clarify the relationship. They may encourage open discussion of the relationship's strengths and weaknesses. The therapist may call unhealthy relationship patterns into question. These could include codependency, emotional abuse, or repeated affairs. Therapists can help people who have been cheated on work through feelings of self-blame.

HELP RECOVERING FROM A PARTNER'S INFIDELITY

Discovering a partner's infidelity can be a big blow. It is natural to feel intense or confusing emotions. Some people choose to speak with a therapist about these feelings. Individual therapy can help someone who has been affected by infidelity. Therapy may help explain a person's response to their partner's affair. It may focus on forgiving, letting go, or moving on. There are many ways to handle feelings that come with infidelity. A therapist can help you look at your options. You might decide to reconcile with or separate from your partner. Therapy can be useful for couples affected by infidelity. Couples therapy can help address the needs of both partners. A couple could choose to save their relationship. Therapy may help them work on their bond. A couple may also choose to break up as a result of infidelity. They may pursue therapy for a more civil breakup.

Couples affected by infidelity may go to discernment counseling. In this type of therapy, the relationship is on the table. Both partners decide whether they want to stay in the relationship. Partners often have opposing wishes when they begin discernment counseling. The therapist can help them come to an agreement. They will help both partners accept the final decision.

THERAPY FOR AVOIDING INFIDELITY

Some people cite lack of fulfillment as a reason for cheating. It may also be sex addiction, low self-esteem, revenge, or something else. Therapy can help with many of these issues. If you feel like cheating on your partner, consider what is causing this desire. You may be able to address it in therapy. This could help you avoid infidelity. One-on-one or couples therapy can help you address dissatisfaction in your relationship. It may also address negative feelings that may be suppressed. Cognitive behavioral therapy (CBT) could help you work through sex addiction.

If you are tempted to engage in infidelity, it may help to be honest about it. Acknowledging the issue and working through it with your partner may be helpful. Honesty may end up lending strength to the relationship.

THE RECOVERY PROCESS

Recovery from an affair can be a lengthy process. It may be especially lengthy for couples that wish to reconcile. There is no way to tell if a couple will recover from an affair. It is impossible

to tell how long recovery may take. But experts agree that healing can often occur within 2 years. Some couples may take longer to recover. Others can mend their relationship sooner.

Again, there is no concrete timeline for recovery. A recovery timeline may depend on a couple's reactions after the affair is discovered.

Other factors can influence the recovery process. These include:

- Communication skills
- Tolerance for conflict
- Capacity for honesty
- Acceptance of personal responsibility
- Attachment style

Every relationship is unique. The process of recovering from infidelity also varies. Recovery

typically progresses through the
following phases:

- **Trauma Phase.** This phase
  comes after the affair is
  discovered. The betrayed
  partner may
  feel shock or trauma when
  they find out about the affair.
  They may feel angry,
  vengeful, and hopeless. This
  phase is often a roller coaster
  of emotions. These can range
  from loss and grief to rage
  and frustration. They can
  come with tears or conflict.
  Both partners struggle with
  thinking clearly during this
  phase. They may experience
  physical symptoms such as

loss of appetite and weight loss.

- **Issues Clarification.** During this time, couples begin to examine what led to the affair. There may still be a great deal of emotional instability. But the partners now want to understand why the affair happened. This process can lead to closure. The sooner couples can begin, the sooner they may reap the rewards of closure. Enlisting the help of a therapist may be helpful during this time. This phase may be stressful to one or both partners.

- **Addressing the Problem.** This is when the real work begins. Emotions become more manageable. Partners can then start working on the issues that led to the affair. There

will be highs and lows in this process. Guilt and anger can mix with longing for the relationship as it once was. But couples can benefit from persevering through this phase. They are often able to address issues at the root their discontent.

Next, couples can embrace the new relationship they have created. Therapy for infidelity can allow couples to grow a stronger and truer bond. But it may still be difficult for the betrayed partner to trust the other. Both partners can still have difficulty understanding why the affair happened. They may have trouble accepting that the life they knew will not be the same.

Techniques taught in therapy can help couples learn how to get over the affair. They can continue to develop an open, honest, and new relationship. This relationship will be freer from the negative emotions of the affair.

Ending a relationship after infidelity

For the person whose partner cheated. A couple might decide to end their relationship after an affair. Therapists can still assist both parties during this time. The partner who was betrayed may find it helpful to discuss feelings of inadequacy, betrayal, and anger. A therapist can also help them cope with the trauma of losing a partner.

For the person who had an affair. The partner who had the affair may feel regret. They may wish to understand what caused them to pursue an affair. For example, they might have had an affair because they felt their relationship was not satisfying. A therapist can help them learn how to share feelings of dissatisfaction more effectively. Learning these skills may prevent them from repeating the behavior.

Consider the process of taking about an affair. There are many steps in that process. Opening up about an affair is one step. Discussing what to do next is another series of talks. These may take time. The final step is often one of two things. It may be a discussion of how to end the relationship. It may also be series of dialogues that revolve around rebuilding trust.

It can be hard to know how to get over an affair. A couple's counselor can help couples at any stage of discussing an affair. The following are some tips to keep in mind during these discussions:

- **Be patient.** If you had an affair, be patient with your partner's reactions. Processing your affair may be painful for them. It can also help to practice patience with your partner if you were cheated on. Let them express how they feel about the situation, as well.

-

-

- **Be responsible.** If you had an affair, your partner may have strong emotions, including anger. Avoid blaming your

partner for your actions.
Don't minimize the impact of
your actions.

- **Apologize and forgive.** This
must happen if a couple
wishes to rebuild their
relationship. The person who
had an affair must offer a
sincere apology. The person
who was cheated on must
accept this apology on solid
terms. This process cannot be
rushed. But it is often
necessary for a relationship to
be rebuilt.

- **Communicate.** Actively
listen to what your partner
has to say. Speak truthfully to
them in return. Reaffirm your

dedication to fixing the relationship, if that is your choice.

- **Deciding to reveal an affair.** Amara, 27, seeks therapy because she has cheated on her partner. She feels guilty. Amara recently ended the affair. But she has not yet revealed her infidelity to her partner. She is terrified of doing this. She does not want this relationship to end. She also does not want to hurt her partner's feelings. Amara feels she "ought" to tell her partner. She is not sure that doing so is the best course. The therapist helps Amara clarify what her motivations for telling or not telling might be. Together, they evaluate the possible consequences of each path. Amara decides that her commitment to honesty requires her to tell her partner. The therapist helps her prepare for this task and manage her anxiety afterwards. Couple's work with a different therapist is recommended to help the pair recover further.

. **Determining whether or not to separate.** Don and Felicia, in their 40s, enter couples counseling. Don has revealed he has a mistress. He is unsure if he is ready to stop seeing her. Felicia is angry and depressed. She feels she should leave the marriage, but she's "still in love with

Don." The therapist forms an agreement with the couple. They will decide whether to continue or dissolve the marriage in one month. Don breaks off his affair. But he is still very ambivalent. The therapist helps the couple uncover long-standing problems with intimacy in their marriage. Don admits to other, previous affairs. Don and Felicia are both recommended for simultaneous, separate individual therapy. Don must work on his compulsions. Felicia must work through feelings of inadequacy and anger. After several months, Felicia decides she needs a trial separation. Don admits he is still having an affair. However, they continue therapy together. Don finally ends his affair. One year later, the couple reunites. They begin picking up the pieces with help from the therapist.

Chapter Six

Rebuilding your Marriage

Infidelity can shatter even the strongest relationship, leaving behind feelings of betrayal, sadness, guilt, uncertainty, and anger. For the married couples who experienced infidelity in their relationship it can be extremely difficulty to both forgive as well as overcome. Although, it may be difficult for partners that have been cheated on to forgive or get beyond the affair once it has been discovered or revealed, it is possible. Partners that are able to put the hurt and betrayal of the affair behind them can emerge as a stronger and more cohesive couple.

Unfortunately, for many couples, the weight of an affair can prove too big to overcome. Whatever the reason for the affair, the effect of infidelity can be devastating on a relationship. Partners that are stuck in their pain and animus following betrayal in their relationship often experience a breakdown of the relationship. Learning how to appropriately communicate thoughts and feelings is an essential first step in getting beyond the pain of an affair.

Understandably, once an affair is discovered partners struggle with understanding why the affair occurred, the signs they missed, what they should have done differently, etc. There are many different reasons why someone might have an affair, reasons that may not be readily available to both the partner that has the affair and the partner that was cheated on. Sometimes it is purely a case of poor judgment — a person may feel satisfied with their marriage, but a late night at the office with a co-worker and a couple of glasses of wine can lead to lack of impulse control. More commonly, it's a search for an emotional connection — wanting someone to pay attention to you, be attracted to you, or compliment you.

Although, personal examination may seem impossible to do following an affair, both partners must examine the role each played in the affair. Examining personal roles in an affair is a delicate dance as it is often hard for the partner cheated on to see his or her role in the affair. The breakdown of communication and intimacy in a relationship lies with both partners, therefore, it is important to engage in personal examination of individual roles to best understand an affair. However, the spouse that had the affair needs to be willing to discuss what happened openly if

the betrayed spouse wants to do that. Understandably, the spouse that has been cheated on may want to talk about the affair in detail, e.g., how his or her partner met the person they cheated with, how long the affair went on, was the individual better than his or her spouse, etc. As difficult as it may seem, the cheating spouse must be willing to answer questions about the affair that are both difficult and uncomfortable.

Affairs have the potential to crack the foundation of a marriage, breakdown communication, and destroy trust. Issues with trust can run so deep following an affair that the individual that cheated has to be willing to be accountable for his or her whereabouts, even though he or she thinks that may be unfair. There needs to be a willingness to make promises and commitments about the future, that an affair will not happen again. Too often, the person that cheated wants to quickly put the affair behind him or her, however, he or she needs to honor the timetable of his or her partner. The person who had the affair must examine the personal reasons for straying and what needs to change to avoid the temptation in the future.

As for moving forward, both people in the relationship should take responsibility for rebuilding trust, improving communication, creating barriers around their relationship, and enhancing intimacy.

Cheating Partners can Heal from The Pain of an Affair by Doing the Following:

Talking about the Affair openly and honestly with your spouse Avoid blaming the person you cheated with for the affair Take ownership of your role in the affair Apologize for the hurt and pain you caused by having an affair Answering questions from your spouse about the affair regardless of your personal comfort Be willing to accept that you may need to give your spouse time to heal from the affair Understand that trust has been broken in the relationship and you may need to account for your whereabouts for a while Create a new meaning of intimacy in

your marriage Work with spouse to create new rules for the marriage Agreeing to have no further contact with the person involved in the affair

Partners Cheated on Can Heal from the Pain of an Affair by Doing the Following:

Avoiding a rush to judgment Forgiving their spouse too quickly Setting new rules in the relationship Ignoring Aphorisms (once a cheater always a cheater) Telling friends and family about the affair, especially, if you have not had the opportunity to process it Assigning the blame of the affair on the individual your spouse cheated with.

Remember your spouse is the one that made the commitment to you, not the person he or she cheated with. Avoid comparing yourself to the other person Understand your role in the affair Redefine Sexual Intimacy Refrain from tit for tat behavior (having an affair to get back at your partner for his or her affair) Rush to seek a divorce Rule out marital counseling Work with spouse to create new rules for the marriage

One of the greatest hurdles in the healing process following an affair lies between the sheets. Often, a couple feels like the other person remains in the middle of their relationship, preventing them from trusting each other, engaging in a healthy display of affection, and waiting for the next opportunity to invade the marriage. The phantom interloper can have dire consequences on the marriage. The unfaithful spouse often feels pressured to please in bed, leading to distraction and low performance, which the hurt party, already injured and insecure, interprets as a lack of interest, desire, and physical attraction. The best way to put an affair behind you and come out stronger is to receive marital/relationship counseling. Counseling allows couples to talk about their relationship and the affair in a non-threatening environment. Spouses can learn the skills needed to improve communication, build trust, enhance intimacy, strengthen the foundation of their relationship, and decrease the likelihood of an affair in the future.

www.ingramcontent.com/pod-product-compliance
Lightning Source LLC
Chambersburg PA
CBHW071443150726
48000CB00006B/2429